HISTORY'S GREATEST WARRIORS

# KNIGHTS

## WARRIORS OF THE MIDDLE AGES

Pliny O'Brian

Cavendish
Square
New York

Published in 2015 by Cavendish Square Publishing, LLC
243 5th Avenue, Suite 136, New York, NY 10016

Library of Congress Cataloging-in-Publication Data

O'Brian, Pliny.
Knights : warriors of the Middle Ages / Pliny O'Brian.
pages cm. — (History's greatest warriors)
Includes index.
ISBN 978-1-50260-120-9 (hardcover) ISBN 978-1-50260-115-5 (ebook)
1. Knights and knighthood—History—To 1500—Juvenile literature. 2. Military art and science—History—Medieval, 500-1500—Juvenile literature. I. Title.

CR4513.O25 2014
940.1—dc23

2014025724

Editor: Amy Hayes
Copy Editor: Cynthia Roby
Art Director: Jeffrey Talbot
Designer: Joseph Macri
Senior Production Manager: Jennifer Ryder-Talbot
Production Editor: David McNamara
Photo Researcher: J8 Media

2

Printed in the United States of America

# CONTENTS

Knights fought on horseback and attempted to cut down their foes from above.

He sits heavily atop his horse. Even with the help of two **pages** it has taken hours to fully dress him in armor. It is just daybreak and his helmet is already hot. He knows that as the day progresses the sun will continue to heat his armor. Tired and hungry from the journey, he has reached the Holy Land. He is here to fight. He is a knight of the **Middle Ages**.

Preparing for battle, other knights on horses line up around him. All sit at the top of a hill preparing to lay siege to the castle below. He grips his **lance** with one hand, his shield in the other. The enemy opens fire—archers shoot arrows from their bows. Most of the arrows miss their marks, but one hits the horse next to him. The animal rears in pain, flinging its rider to the ground. Then comes the signal.

The knight kicks his horse hard and races toward the enemy. Riding with a tide of knights, he points his lance toward the enemy and strikes an opponent. The lance breaks. The knight then pulls out his sword, cutting down his enemies as his horse gallops frantically through the fight. An enemy soldier pierces the knight's horse with his sword. It falls over in pain.

Getting to his feet, the knight thrusts his sword into his opponent's side. He has reached the Holy Land, and he intends to conquer it.

St. George fights and kills a dragon in one of the most beloved tales of knights of the Middle Ages.

# THE DAWN OF KNIGHTHOOD

Many stories of daring deeds and bravery surround the Middle Ages. Princes and princesses, damsels in distress, beautiful stone castles, and even noble outlaws are all part of the lore of Medieval Europe. You may have heard of Robin Hood and King Arthur. Even some of the historical figures of the time are wrapped in tales of glory. However, no one is more revered than the medieval knight. The idea of chivalrous knights protecting the innocent has always been an essential part of the myths of the Middle Ages.

The myths surrounding knights, however, are wrong. Knights of the

Charlemagne, the Holy Roman Emperor, rides atop a white horse.

Middle Ages were trained killers ready to fight at a moment's notice. They often slaughtered those who didn't share their religious beliefs. Sometimes they kidnapped their enemies and demanded money for their release. Many knights looked to conquer villages and collect their treasures. Knights were both brutal and heroic—not good or bad, but a mixture of both.

# CHARLEMAGNE'S CAVALRY

In the sixth century, with the Roman Empire in ruins, much of Europe was unguarded. Ruthless invaders ransacked towns, and local warriors decided to battle back. These were considered the first knights. They were usually free peasants who simply wanted to defend their homes from attack. As they gained more success, their legend grew.

Soon, great leaders began to hear tales of these warriors' daring acts of bravery. A powerful king and emperor, Charlemagne, helped to organize the knights. Charlemagne ruled most of Western Europe in the eighth century. His kingdom came under attack, mostly by Saxons, a tribe from central Germany. Worried that the invaders threatened his rule, Charlemagne formed a **cavalry** to destroy his enemies. As word of their deeds spread throughout Europe, the legend of these knights began to grow.

# FEUDALISM BEGINS

After Charlemagne's death in 814, his Empire began to crumble. The government was left too weak to protect its citizens. Thieves and bandits attacked towns at will. Landowners lived in constant fear of invasion. They didn't have enough money to pay soldiers, but they desperately needed protection. To help protect their land, they created a system called **feudalism**. Under feudalism, people were given land in exchange for goods or services. A king or lord who owned land would offer a portion of it to a knight and his family. In return, knights defended kings, lords, and their lands on the battlefield.

## SQUIRE'S TIP

Sometimes knights were loyal to whomever offered the most money.

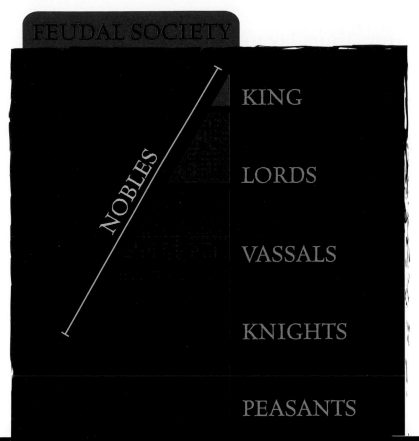

FEUDAL SOCIETY

NOBLES

KING

LORDS

VASSALS

KNIGHTS

PEASANTS

Feudal society was shaped like a pyramid: there were many peasants at the bottom of the pyramid, and only one king at the top.

## A BOND WITH THE CHURCH

The Catholic Church took note of the knights' heroic feats. Church leaders were impressed by the knights' bravery, but worried about their targets. Some were attacking monks and priests. The church wrote a document called the "Truce of God," which asked knights not to fight from Thursday to Sunday. It ordered the warriors not to attack religious places. The church convinced knights to protect it, not harm it.

Priests and monks promised knights that their bravery would be rewarded. If the knights fought for the church, they would be guaranteed a place in heaven. Knights were ordered to draw their swords only against the enemies of the church.

## CHRISTIAN CRUSADERS

Cooperation between knights and the church reached a high point during the **Crusades**. The Crusades were a series of wars fought between European Christians and Muslims living in areas near the Mediterranean Sea. The wars lasted from 1096 to 1270.

By the eighth century, Muslim forces had taken control of North Africa, the eastern Mediterranean, and most of Spain. In 1071, a group of Muslims called Seljuk Turks captured the Middle Eastern city of Jerusalem. This city was a

Religious knights often fought with the Christian cross as their flag. The red cross on a white background was the sign of the Knights Templar.

holy place throughout Europe, Asia, and Africa. Christians living in the Middle East were often robbed and beaten by the Seljuk Turks.

Pope Urban II, head of the Catholic Church, believed that Christians had a right to the Holy Land of Jerusalem. He called on knights to take back Jerusalem from the Muslims. In 1096, more than 4,000 knights began the battle to win the city back.

Fierce and bloody, the First Crusade was also a success. In 1099, the knights captured Jerusalem. They showed no mercy toward their conquered enemies, slaughtering the Turks.

## TURMOIL IN THE HOLY LAND

Many other Crusades followed. Control of the Holy Land passed back and forth between Christians and Muslims—both sides believing that God wanted them to have power over the area. Each Crusade was extremely bloody and resulted in huge losses of life.

For European knights, life in the Middle East ended in bloody battles. Many died off the field as well, succumbing to disease and hunger. Crusaders did not understand these failures—they believed that controlling Jerusalem was a holy quest and that God was on their side. They also believed that fighting for the Holy Land would get them into heaven.

## THE KNIGHTS OF KING ARTHUR

Tales from the Middle Ages were often of magic and wizardry. Many of these tales praised knights. The most famous legend combined both knighthood and magic: the legend of King Arthur. According to myth, Arthur ruled a land called Camelot. He fought evil with his magic sword, named Excalibur.

One story tells that, as a boy, Arthur was the only one able to remove Excalibur from the stone in which it was stuck.

Arthur was crowned king, and married the lovely Guinevere.

King Arthur led a cavalry of twenty-eight knights. These heroic fighters were known as the Knights of the Round Table. Each knight was given his seat at the table for the daring and brave deeds he did. The knights helped spread peace throughout the land, and united England as one country for the first time.

Even though most of the stories of King Arthur are fiction, he was much revered throughout the Middle Ages.

Pages and squires helped knights with daily duties in the hopes that, one day, they too would become knights.

# CHAPTER TWO

# A LIFE IN ARMS

## STARTING YOUNG

Knights started learning their skills early. Many started training at the tender age of four. These young boys learned how to ride gentle ponies. As the boys grew older, they would be given positions as pages.

A page served the lord of the castle, performing errands. During their free time, pages learned to hunt animals with a spear and a bow. Using blunt, wooden swords, they sharpened their skills for future battles. They also used small, round shields called bucklers.

*The Vigil*, by John Pettie, shows a squire praying before his knighting ceremony.

At fourteen, a talented page was promoted to **squire**. Each squire assisted one knight. Squires performed a variety of chores, from serving meals to cleaning swords. Squires followed their knight everywhere—even on the battlefield. If the knight lost a weapon while in battle, the squire rushed into combat to replace it.

After learning these skills, squires were knighted. Squires remained awake the night before their knighting ceremonies. They prayed until morning in a church, refusing to eat or sleep. At dawn, they took a long bath and dressed in a white linen robe. At the ceremony, a squire swore to use his sword only for God. His lord would then tap the flat edge of a sword against him. At this point, the squire was dubbed, or knighted.

## SHINING ARMOR

Knights covered themselves from head to toe in armor. They also wore a short tunic called a hauberk. Hauberks were made of **chain mail** and draped over the neck. Chain mail was constructed of up to forty thousand tiny links of metal. Hauberks protected knights from having their necks slashed open by enemy swords. By the late Middle Ages, knights began wearing a plate of armor over the chain mail. Armor plates prevented arrows from piercing the knights' bodies.

This armor was worn by a German knight in the 1500s. It was specifically designed for fighting while on horseback.

# WEAPONS AND TACTICS

Weapons were an essential part of battle. Each knight carried a kite-shaped shield in his left hand, while holding his sword with his right. At the start of the Middle Ages, knights used double-edged swords and slashed at their foes. Later on, the sword was built to be stronger and stiffer. A new diamond-shaped tip allowed knights to stab the enemy through their links of chain mail. Knights also used axes, daggers, and falchions. A falchion is a weapon that looked like a butcher's cleaver.

The warhorses that knights rode into battle, or **destriers**, were bred specifically for combat. To attack his enemy, a knight raised himself up on his warhorse, almost to a standing position. He held his lance beside him. Then the destrier galloped toward the knight's enemy. Both knight and horse turned into a kind of living missile. While charging, the knight tried to stab the enemy with his lance.

Double edged swords, axes, and maces were common weapons used by the Medieval knights.

# TOURNEYS AND PRACTICE

During peacetime, knights competed in tournaments to keep their battle skills sharp. People traveled from far and wide to watch these events. Until about 1200, tournaments often took the form of a **melee**, meaning that knights fought one another in hand-to-hand combat. During these mock battles they even took one another hostage. While melees thrilled tournament spectators, they were very dangerous for the warriors. The fierce fighting often got out of hand, leading to injuries and even deaths. Rules were made to make the events safer. Tournament judges limited the places where knights could hit each other with their weapons.

## A COAT OF ARMS

On the battlefield, knights wore armor that completely covered their faces. This made recognizing each other difficult. A system called "heraldry" fixed this problem. Heraldry was a practice in which a pattern or design was inscribed on the knight's shield. Each noble family had a basic pattern and set of colors. A family's eldest son inherited the design, called a coat of arms.

## SQUIRE'S TIP

If a man married into a rich family, he might add his wife's coat of arms to his own.

A heraldic roll was a collection of coats of arms. This is part of the Segar's Roll, created in 1282.

## A CODE OF CHIVALRY

Knights lived by a certain code. The code demanded that they defend the weak and live an honorable life. Part of the code included **chivalry**—a type of polite and noble behavior, shown especially toward women. During medieval times, chivalry became a very romantic ideal. Once a knight fell in love with a woman, he worshipped her in the name of chivalry. He dedicated his battles to her. In return, she praised his courage.

Often, a woman would show her love for a knight by giving him a token, usually an item of clothing such as a scarf, to wear during tournaments. Knights would wear these tokens close to their hearts as they rode into battle.

The affection and loyalty these knights showed these women concerned the Catholic Church. Priests worried that women would distract knights from their duty to defend the church. However, the knights ignored the church's protests. Love prevailed, and the code of chivalry continued.

Albrect Dürer's *The Knight on Horseback and the Lansquenet* shows a knight upon his destrier and a German foot soldier.

# CHAPTER THREE

# WEAPONS AND BATTLES

At the beginning of battle, the cavalry would line up on horseback and charge the enemy all at once. This tactic, called **conrois**, was used to break enemy lines. It was a terrifying sight—a line of knights, lances in hand, forcefully charging toward an enemy. The cavalry could not turn around or back up, so they only had one chance to use this tactic. They always made sure it was as effective as possible.

Lances weren't the only weapons knights used while charging on their destriers. They also used swords to slash through their enemies' chain mail. While it wasn't easy to control the weapons, large knobs at the end of the sword's handle, called pommels, helped. Pommels kept the swords balanced, allowing knights to control them as they slashed at flesh and metal.

Knights also struck their enemies with heavy maces. A mace was a heavy club with a spiked, metal head. The weapon was every bit as deadly as swords and lances. Knights swung these clubs like baseball bats, brutally striking their enemies. A well-placed blow could split a foe's skull or crush his bones.

## CASTLE SIEGE

Often during the Middle Ages, invaders tried to take over castles. Knights tasked with protecting a castle would charge the invaders before they reached its gates. Some invaders were taken hostage, while others were killed. Unfortunately, it wasn't always possible for knights to beat invaders to the punch.

Sometimes invaders managed to surround a castle, where they often remained outside for days, even months, in hopes

Castle sieges could take a very long time. Sometimes knights would attempt to climb the high castle walls.

that the knights and lords would starve to death. When this happened, residents had to make sure their castle was well-stocked with food. Some attackers even dug beneath castle walls to get inside.

## SQUIRE'S TIP

Some battles were bloodier than others. There were times when the cavalry would run low on knights. Squires would dash in with swords of their own during these emergencies.

## RICHARD THE LIONHEART

The Third Crusade made a hero out of England's Richard the Lionheart. Though Richard lost the Crusade, he signed an important treaty with the Turks in 1192. The treaty won Christians the right to continue **pilgrimages** to the Holy Land.

In all, there were eight Crusades which spanned over two hundred years. Control over the Holy Land shifted back and forth until 1244. At that point, Muslims took control of Jerusalem for the final time. By the end of the thirteenth century, the crusading Christians and knights had been driven out of the area.

Richard the Lionheart (right) about to fight Phillip II at the Battle of Gisors.

## MUSLIM MEDICINE

Medieval warfare took a gruesome toll on a knight's body. In their armor, crusaders sweltered in the desert climate of the Middle East. Others suffered from hunger and disease. Knights didn't have doctors to help them, or hospitals in which to recover. Europeans then knew very little about medicine. As a result, many knights died of battle wounds. Muslims, however, knew much more about medicine.

European physicians learned a lot from Muslim doctors in the Middle East.

Knights first refused to trust Muslim knowledge. However, by the fifteenth century, Europeans had begun practicing Muslim ways of healing. Some historians say that this sharing of knowledge was one of the few good things to come from the Crusades.

## MILITARY ORDERS

During the Crusades, many knights joined religious military orders. Knights founded these orders to combine charity, faith, and bravery on the battlefield. Three of the most famous orders were the Templar Knights, the Hospitalers, and the Teutonic Knights.

The Templar Knights were known for their banking skills, having invented a system of depositing money in one town and using it in another. This was an early version of a checking account.

The Hospitalers started out with a mission of helping sick pilgrims. Soon they began defending the Holy Land as well.

The Teutonic Knights were involved in trade and politics. They converted many people to Christianity.

Both the Hospitalers and the Teutonic Knights remain in existence today as charitable organizations that help the sick and less fortunate. The Templars met a darker fate. By the fourteenth century, the Templars had become very powerful. Worried about the level of power the Templars held, the Catholic Church spread rumors that the order worshipped the devil. People quickly turned against the Templars, and many of these powerful knights were burned at the stake.

Caoursin, seated in the golden chair, was the Vice-Chancellor of the Order of the Hospitalers.

Archers, with their longbows, were much more efficient and deadly during a siege than knights.

# CHAPTER FOUR

# A LEGACY OF CHIVALRY

After the thirteenth century, knights began to face a foe they couldn't defeat: progress. Approaches to combat were forever altered with the development of **longbows** and **crossbows**, which changed how battles were fought. During the Hundred Years' War (1337–1453), steel-tip arrows, flying up to a quarter of a mile, ripped through medieval armor. Knights didn't stand a chance against archery tactics.

Foot soldiers created another new weapon in the fourteenth century called a "halberd." These long axes were topped with curved spikes. When knights charged a soldier carrying a halberd, they often met a gruesome end. Their enemy would catch them with the curve of the axe, splitting their skulls.

Once gunpowder was introduced to Western Europe in the fourteenth century, the knights' era was all but over. Cannons and guns turned out to be far more deadly than an entire cavalry. These new weapons not only did more damage than swords and lances, they were also more accurate. The skills of knights were no match for these new ways of warfare.

## SQUIRE'S TIP

Charles VII of France formed Europe's first professional army in 1415. During the battle of Agincourt, he witnessed his cavalry cornered and killed by archers. It was then that he realized the days of the knights were over.

## RETREAT FROM BATTLE

Knights began living on large estates, rather than at the king's castle. Many preferred living the life of a gentleman to fighting wars. Wealthy knights often paid artists and poets to create works for them.

The knights' wealthy lifestyle soon became harder to maintain. They were making less money than merchants and farmers, since nobles no longer took to the battlefield. Peasants did the fighting instead. Knights steadily lost their influence with kings. Yet by the fifteenth century, chivalry was still embraced. It now had little to do with battlefield bravery and was more an ideal of how to behave in public. People displayed suits of armor for show, not battle.

## RENAISSANCE FAIRES

In recent years, groups have tried to bring medieval history back to life. People dress up in chain mail and carry weapons once used by knights. They hold **jousting** events, tournaments, and more. These groups perform for delighted audiences across the world.

Tourneys are still held today to honor knights of the past, and imagine what the Middle Ages must have been like.

For many years, films, television programs, and books have captured the magic of chivalry and knighthood. These works of art entertain and delight audiences and readers. They also inform people about the myths and legends of chivalry.

## HONORIFIC ORDERS

The code of chivalry for which knights stood remains honored today. Each year, the Queen of England chooses people who have made a great impact on society to receive the title of knighthood. Politicians, surgeons, and entertainers have won this honor. Former president of South Africa Nelson Mandela and film director Steven Spielberg are among those who have been granted honorary knighthood status. Women who are honored receive the title of dame.

Knights no longer head into battle. The days of Crusades, melees, and tourneys are over. However, the idea of those noble warriors still lives on in the hearts and minds of people today. Thus, the medieval knight will forever be considered an emblem of the Middle Ages.

Here, the Queen of England knights the New Zealand Governor-General Anand Satyanand.

**cavalry** Soldiers who fight on horseback.

**chain mail** Flexible armor made of several linked metal rings.

**chivalry** A code of noble and polite behavior that was expected of a medieval knight.

**conrois** A battle tactic during which the entire cavalry charges the enemy at once.

**crossbow** A weapon with a bow mounted across a piece of wood.

**Crusades** Battles fought in the eleventh, twelfth, and thirteenth centuries by European Christians attempting to capture biblical lands from Muslims.

**destrier** A knight's steed, or war horse.

**feudalism** The medieval system in which people were given land and protection by the owner of the land, or lord, and in return worked and fought for him.

**jousting**  A battle between two knights riding horses and armed with lances.

**lance**  A long weapon, usually a wooden shaft and a pointed steel head, used for thrusting. Lances were once used by a horseman in charging enemies.

**longbow**  A hand-drawn wooden bow held vertically.

**melee**  A hand-to-hand fight among several people.

**Middle Ages**  The period in European history from the collapse of Roman civilization in the fifth century CE to the period of the Renaissance.

**page**  A boy who served as a knight's personal servant.

**pilgrimage**  A journey to worship at a holy place.

**squire**  A young nobleman who helped a knight and accompanied him into battle.

# Books

Gravett, Christopher. *Knight*. DK Eyewitness Books. New York, NY: DK Children, 2007.

Harkins, Susan, and William H. Harkins. *The Life and Times of King Arthur: The Evolution of the Legend*. Biography from Ancient Civilizations: Legends, Folklore, and Stories of Ancient Worlds. Newark, DE: Mitchell Lane Publishers, 2006.

Hepplewhite, Peter. *Knights*. Greatest Warriors. London, UK: Arcturus Publishing, 2013.

Steele, Philip. *A Knight's City*. New York, NY: Little Simon, 2008.

# Websites

**British Library, Medieval Realms**
www.bl.uk/learning/histcitizen/medieval/
medievalrealms.html

This website by the British Library displays primary source paintings and illustrations of aspects of medieval life. Take a photographic tour of the towns, rural life, food, medicines, monsters, and more.

**The History Channel "Crusades"**
www.history.com/topics/crusades

The History Channel's official site provides an overview of the Crusades, as well as short videos of reenactments.

**The Middle Ages, Western Reserve Public Media**
westernreservepublicmedia.org/middleages/feud_
knights.htm

Discover the structure of the society of the Middle Ages, and learn more about how young men became knights. There are games, videos, and links to websites that explore medieval culture.